Human Capital and the Future of the Gulf

AUTHOR
Carolyn Barnett

November 2015

A Report of the CSIS Middle East Program

CSIS | CENTER FOR STRATEGIC &
INTERNATIONAL STUDIES

ROWMAN &
LITTLEFIELD

Lanham • Boulder • New York • London

About CSIS

For over 50 years, the Center for Strategic and International Studies (CSIS) has worked to develop solutions to the world's greatest policy challenges. Today, CSIS scholars are providing strategic insights and bipartisan policy solutions to help decisionmakers chart a course toward a better world.

CSIS is a nonprofit organization headquartered in Washington, D.C. The Center's 220 full-time staff and large network of affiliated scholars conduct research and analysis and develop policy initiatives that look into the future and anticipate change.

Founded at the height of the Cold War by David M. Abshire and Admiral Arleigh Burke, CSIS was dedicated to finding ways to sustain American prominence and prosperity as a force for good in the world. Since 1962, CSIS has become one of the world's preeminent international institutions focused on defense and security; regional stability; and transnational challenges ranging from energy and climate to global health and economic integration.

Former U.S. senator Sam Nunn has chaired the CSIS Board of Trustees since 1999. Former deputy secretary of defense John J. Hamre became the Center's president and chief executive officer in 2000.

CSIS does not take specific policy positions; accordingly, all views expressed herein should be understood to be solely those of the author(s).

ISBN: 978-1-4422-5904-1 (pb); 978-1-4422-5905-8 (eBook)

Center for Strategic & International Studies
1616 Rhode Island Avenue, NW
Washington, DC 20036
202-887-0200 | *www.csis.org*

Rowman & Littlefield
4501 Forbes Boulevard
Lanham, MD 207066
301-459-3366 | *www.rowman.com*

Contents

Human Capital and the Future of the Gulf

Carolyn Barnett

Executive Summary

Extensive efforts to develop human capital are under way in the United Arab Emirates, Saudi Arabia, and elsewhere in the Gulf, and they are increasingly setting expectations for how people ought to behave socially and economically that are in tension with how they are expected to behave politically.

In their efforts to build "knowledge economies," Gulf governments have invested heavily in education. They have recently begun to place greater emphasis on career guidance, technical and vocational education, and entrepreneurship. These efforts are as much an attempt to change attitudes and expectations around work and productivity as an attempt to build skills or change incentives. Yet in order for states to make full use of the human capital in which they are investing, they want citizens to embrace proactive attitudes and be economically and socially innovative. This drive for innovation occurs in a constrained political context in which deference to and reverence for authority remain the expectation, and in which challenging social norms can be difficult. There is a clear tension between countries' wish to encourage economic creativity and risk taking on the one hand, and their desire to maintain relative social and political quiescence on the other. Navigating this tension—or finding ways to create space for genuine innovation and risk taking within that constrained political context—will be among the most important strategic challenges for the region's leaders and people in the next 10 years.

The tensions created by governments' conflicting aims can produce frustration, a sense of entitlement, or apathy among young people entering the labor force, each of which poses different potential political challenges for governments, although most Gulf states do not face threats to their basic stability. Some young people whose ambitions are being constrained have grown frustrated, and they

There is a clear tension between countries' wish to encourage economic creativity and risk taking on the one hand, and their desire to maintain relative social and political quiescence on the other.

are using their new skills and tools to push where they can for social change or different policies. In others, a sense of entitlement is reinforced, and this will increase the difficulty of shifting expectations about the respective roles of the state and citizens in the future. Meanwhile, governments continue to search for good strategies to change the behavior of the disengaged and underachieving. Alienation and apathy among potentially productive citizens undermine governments' goals for economic growth and contribute to other social ills, including poor health, crime, and possible susceptibility to recruitment by radical groups.

Changes are happening in the Gulf. Both government efforts and grassroots mobilization are starting to promote the idea that governments and citizens should celebrate risk, encourage public service, and push for more local creation of knowledge for future policymaking.

These trends may simultaneously reinforce acceptance of the basic political status quo and give people new tools and incentives to seek greater economic and social change within it. Change may also alienate important beneficiaries of present systems, who have economic and political stakes in maintaining the status quo.

Governments are confronting the fundamental question of whether it is possible for them to shift the expectations and obligations underpinning their political systems without breaking those systems. Some people expect to see a "Big Bang" in the region— but a slow evolution is more likely. Yet even incremental changes have consequences. How tensions and expectations around work and employment evolve, and how governments respond to these shifts, will be a major variable in the region's politics. ●

Introduction

One winter afternoon in Dubai, 16 young Emirati men attended a workshop on leadership, teamwork, and empowerment in a hotel conference room. Dressed alternatively in traditional Emirati robes or in jeans and t-shirts, some slumped low in their seats, while others sat alert. At the front of the room, another young Emirati energetically scribbled on an easel as the participants shared words that they associated with qualities of leadership: Strength. Vision. Confidence. Wisdom.

"Who embodies these qualities? Who do you look up to as a model for leadership?" the moderator asked.

One by one, the young men soberly volunteered their responses. The range was limited. Every single participant cited either the Prophet Muhammad or one of the current ruling figures of the United Arab Emirates (UAE).[1] These men, they noted, demonstrated the qualities they identified with true leadership.

The participants had voluntarily joined a day-long workshop (offered by a semigovernmental institution) geared toward helping Emirati youth develop their leadership skills, mentorship skills, and employability.[2] Pushing themselves to think unconventionally was ostensibly why the participants were there in the first place, but no one felt empowered to buck the consensus by citing a pioneering businessman or even a personal relative. To depart from the consensus seemed to represent disloyalty at best.

---

[1] These included Sheikh Khalifa bin Zayed Al-Nahyan (current ruler of Abu Dhabi and president of the UAE), Sheikh Muhammad bin Zayed Al-Nahyan (crown prince of Abu Dhabi), and Sheikh Muhammad bin Rashed Al-Maktoum (ruler of Dubai).
[2] Across the hall, around two dozen young women were going through the same set of leadership and team-building exercises.

In their enthusiasm for learning new skills, this group of young people represented the success of efforts to promote human capital development in the UAE.[3] Similar efforts have been ongoing in other countries of the Gulf Cooperation Council (GCC). Educating young people to be active participants in their society reflects broader strategic goals that governments in the region have set for themselves. Government strategy documents across the region have for years emphasized the need not only to diversify economies and boost private sector employment, but also to promote the development of citizens able to build and advance "knowledge economies" for the twenty-first century.[4] The concept of a "knowledge economy" is often left vaguely defined or even undefined in policy discussions—possibly because few have a clear idea of what it will look like in the Gulf context. Broadly, what most people mean is that the nation's wealth and productivity will come from sectors that require innovation, creativity, and the input of well-educated and well-trained individuals, rather than from hydrocarbon wealth.

For a long time, employment has been a key mechanism for distributing that wealth. States sell hydrocarbons, collect the money, and employ their citizens in disproportionate numbers. Although governments have tinkered with and half-heartedly tried to reform this setup over the past few decades, little has changed.[5] The lackluster outcomes of past reform efforts lead some observers to argue that there will be little change in Gulf economies without a fundamental overhaul of the "social contract" in the Gulf. In other words, governments will have to cut off the gravy train, and in the absence of those benefits—with more to gain from having a greater say and less to lose from provoking government ire—populations will probably demand greater political participation.

In the long run, whether that transition is inevitable is an open question. But in the short run, the important question is what sort of social and political changes we might see while the basic arrangement between governments and citizens remains as it is.

Investments in education and expanded promotion of career guidance, technical and vocational education, and entrepreneurship are increasingly setting expecta-

[3] Human capital is loosely defined here as the cumulative capacity of an individual or population to create economic value. It thus encompasses educational opportunities and outcomes, the ability to be productively employed, and less tangible factors or "soft skills" like work ethic, creativity, and entrepreneurship. Governments sometimes also use the term "human resources," al-mawarid al-bashariyya.
[4] See for example Qatar General Secretariat for Development Planning, Qatar National Vision 2030 (July 2008), http://www.gsdp.gov.qa/portal/page/portal/gsdp_en/qatar_national_vision/qnv_2030_document/QNV2030_English_v2.pdf; Qatar Ministry of Education, Qatar Education and Training Sector Strategy 2011–2016: Executive Summary (2012), http://www.sec.gov.qa/En/about/Documents/Stratgy2012E.pdf; Government of Abu Dhabi, The Abu Dhabi Economic Vision 2030 (2008), https://gsec.abudhabi.ae/Sites/GSEC/Content/EN/PDF/Publications/economic-vision-2030-full-version,property=pdf.pdf; Saudi Arabia Ministry of Economy & Planning, The Eighth Development Plan, 2005–2009; Abu Dhabi Competitiveness Report: Improving the Competitiveness of the Emirate of Abu Dhabi (Competitiveness Office of Abu Dhabi, 2013); Saudi Aramco Corporate Citizenship Report 2012 (Saudi Aramco, 2012).

tions for how people will behave socially and economically that are in tension with how they are expected to behave politically. In order for states to make full use of the human capital in which they are investing, they need citizens with resourcefulness and initiative who will be economically and socially innovative. Yet politically, deference to and reverence for authority remain the expectation, and challenging social norms can be difficult in closed political systems.

Some observers expect that the combination of these circumstances will be incendiary. Consider, for example, the first waves of Saudi students returning from study abroad through the King Abdullah Scholarship Program (KASP). The changes to the way they view themselves and their society are stark enough that one Saudi education expert observed, "Our 'Big Bang' has just started...we don't know anything about this society. Things are surprising me everywhere."

This paper analyzes how human capital development efforts implemented to address labor market and economic concerns have produced some changes to young people's attitudes and expectations without any broader overhaul of the social contract. It suggests that these changes will nonetheless shape how politics evolve. It draws on the literature about Gulf labor markets—specifically discussions of distortions in those markets, policies that could address these distortions, and the various obstacles to reform—as well as conversations in the UAE and Saudi Arabia with educators, students, entrepreneurs, government officials, and other expert observers of Gulf business and economics.[6]

The tension between changing attitudes and unchanging structures can produce frustration, a sense of entitlement, or apathy. Each poses different potential political challenges for governments, though none rise to the level of threats to governments' basic stability. Some whose ambitions are constrained grow frustrated, and they may use new their new skills and tools to push from below for social change

[5] The literature on this subject is large, and scholars have approached the topic from many different angles both regionally and with a focus on specific countries. Some of the best recent analyses include Steffen Hertog, "Arab Gulf States: An Assessment of Nationalisation Policies" (Gulf Labor Markets and Migration Research Paper No. 1/2014, Migration Policy Centre, Florence, Italy, 2014); Kasim Randeree, "Workforce Nationalization in the Gulf Cooperation Council States" (Center for International and Regional Studies Occasional Paper No. 9, Georgetown SFS-Qatar, 2012); Steffen Hertog, "A Comparative Assessment of Labor Market Nationalization Policies in the GCC," in *National Employment, Migration, and Education in the GCC*, ed. Steffen Hertog (Berlin: Gerlach Press, 2012), accessed through LSE Online; Martin Baldwin-Edwards, "Labour Immigration and Labour Markets in the GCC Countries: Regional Trends and Patterns" (London School of Economics, Kuwait Programme, March 2011); Ingo Forstenlechner and Emilie Rutledge, "Unemployment in the Gulf: Time to Update the 'Social Contract,'" *Middle East Policy* 17 no. 2 (2010): 38–51; Nabih Maroun and Hatem Samman, *How to Succeed at Education Reform: The Case for Saudi Arabia and the Broader GCC Region* (Booz Allen Hamilton, 2008); Gassan Al-Kibsi, Jorg Schubert, and Claus Benkert, "Getting Labor Policy to Work in the Gulf," *McKinsey Quarterly 2007 Special Edition: Reappraising the Gulf States*.
[6] With Jon B. Alterman, I spoke with dozens of people in the UAE and Saudi Arabia who work in education, human resources, youth empowerment, or other public and private sector institutions concerned with how to build human capital. Unless otherwise cited, quotations throughout this report are from interviews conducted by the author and Jon B. Alterman in the UAE in November 2013 and in Saudi Arabia in January 2014. When particular factual information from an interview is used, the interview is cited, but other quotations are identified in the text itself by the type of individual who shared his or her opinion. Citations of individuals who are not public figures have been anonymized.

or different policies. In others, a sense of entitlement is reinforced, which will increase the difficulty of shifting expectations about the respective roles of the state and citizens in the future. Meanwhile, governments continue to search for good strategies to change the behavior of the disengaged and underachieving. Alienation and disengagement among potentially productive citizens undermine governments' goals for economic growth and contribute to other social ills, including poor health, crime, and possible susceptibility to recruitment by radical groups.

However, the processes under way do not amount to a Big Bang; they are closer to a slow evolution. It is most likely that incremental changes in education and employment patterns will proceed without inducing dramatic political change. In part, this is because governments (some more than others) have intentionally worked to cultivate loyalty, gratitude, and buy-in to existing political arrangements. In some instances, governments are looking for ways to incorporate more citizen input into policy planning and implementation. The broader regional political context has reinforced these efforts by limiting opportunities and reducing incentives for people to demand political change. Regional instability and the threat of domestic terrorism have made many people increasingly willing to accept the political status quo for fear of what might replace it. And in other cases, repressive responses to the Arab uprisings have simply removed avenues through which activists might pursue political change, even as social and economic transformations continue. Meanwhile, though some countries are cutting back on public sector hiring, they have also raised some salaries or expanded other social benefits, despite dropping oil prices. Their actions show that governments can manipulate which elements of the social contract they squeeze and when, even as changes in attitudes around education and work evolve separately.

By design, if efforts to develop human capital are effective, they will alter citizens' expectations and attitudes with regards to their social and economic roles. Those changes could in turn change how some people seek to relate to their governments, though those who do want change will find promoting social and economic transformation much easier than promoting political transformation. Whatever the outcomes, this tension will be a driver of the region's politics moving forward.

Building Human Capital in the Gulf

Investments in Education

The central focus of efforts to advance human capital in the Gulf has been investments in education. The first formal schools in the region opened in the early twentieth century, and less than fifty years ago, more than half the people in the Gulf were illiterate.[7] As across the rest of the Middle East, educational infrastructure and access expanded rapidly through the latter half of the twentieth century.[8] Governments have spent billions of dollars on educational infrastructure, and billions more staffing schools, often with Arab expatriates from other parts of the region. Saudi Arabia has consistently allocated 17–20 percent of its total government expenditure to education,[9] and salaries for teachers comprise more than 80 percent of the Ministry of Education's general budget.[10] UAE data show that more than 20 percent of total government expenditure has been devoted to education for more than a decade.[11] Other GCC governments have devoted between 8 percent and 20 percent of total expenditure to education over the past two decades.[12]

Despite these investments, improved quality of education has not always followed. Gulf students' performance on internationally comparative exams in math and reading, such as the Programme for International Student Assessment (PISA) and the Trends in International Mathematics and Science Study (IMSS) tests show most students perform below the global average.[13] Over the years, governments have announced and launched various reform strategies to try to improve educational quality, and more are under way today.

In the UAE, policymakers have turned to quality of education as the next developmental milestone to tackle. The UAE's Ministry of Education, the Abu Dhabi Education Council (ADEC), and the Knowledge and Human Development Authority (KHDA) in Dubai are the main entities that determine and carry out education reforms. Abu Dhabi and Dubai have un-

---

[7] Into the 1970s, illiteracy rates in the much of the GCC were over 50 percent, according to UNESCO and figures from GCC ministries of education. On the early development of Gulf educational systems, see Natasha Ridge, *Education and the Reverse Gender Divide in the Gulf States: Embracing the Global, Ignoring the Local* (New York: Teachers College Press, 2014), 9–40.

[8] William A. Rugh, "Arab Education: Tradition, Growth and Reform," *Middle East Journal* 56, no. 3 (Summer 2002): 396–414.

[9] World Bank, "Public Spending on Education, Total (% of government expenditure)," http://data.worldbank.org/.

[10] Information on salaries is based on interviews with multiple education sector experts in Saudi Arabia; see also Sharif M. Taha, "86.5% of Education Budget Spent on Paying Salaries," *Arab News*, January 15, 2014, http://www.arabnews.com/news/509331. However, the ministry of education also recently announced a new 80 billion riyal investment in education on top of the ministry's normal budget; it will be devoted to improving infrastructure, training teachers, and other initiatives. "Saudi Arabia Approves $21 bln 5-Year Education Plan," Reuters, May 19, 2014, http://www.reuters.com/article/2014/05/19/saudi-education-idUSL6N0O53HU20140519.

[11] UAE National Qualifications Authority, "The UAE Education System: Overview of Performance in Education" (2013), 11, www.nqa.gov.ae/.../The%20UAE%20Education%20System%20Report.pdf.

[12] World Bank, "Public Spending on Education, Total (% of government expenditure)," http://data.worldbank.org/.

[13] Roberta Pennington, "Quality Is the Biggest Challenge Facing the UAE Educational System," *National*, January 16, 2014, http://www.thenational.ae/uae/education/quality-is-the-biggest-challenge-facing-uaes-education; Michael Barber, Mona Mourshed, and Fenton Whelan, "Improving Education in the Gulf," *McKinsey Quarterly*, April 2007, https://abujoori.files.wordpress.com/2007/04/improve-gulf-education.pdf.

dertaken significant curricular reforms in their government school systems.[14] For example, ADEC this year introduced reforms to curricula in the final years of high school in order to place greater emphasis on science, technology, engineering, and math (STEM). ADEC has previously implemented reforms to the English-language curriculum to strengthen the language skills with which students graduate. One goal of curriculum reform is to ensure that students who arrive at university are prepared for the demands of university-level coursework. Currently the majority of UAE students attending federal universities require at least a year—if not more—in remedial coursework. Some students need two or even three years of remediation.[15] The UAE has also actively encouraged and shaped the emergence of one of the most diverse private educational ecosystems in the world—one that Emiratis themselves are opting into in increasing numbers.[16]

Saudi Arabia rewrote its school curricula in the 2000s, partly in response to concerns that schools were inculcating radicalism. Yet in Saudi Arabia (as elsewhere across the region), schools still emphasize rote memorization, and they focus as much on instilling religious discipline as on imparting practical knowledge. Reform efforts are ongoing: in mid-2014, the country announced an additional planned $21 billion investment in education, and later that year the Ministry of Labor launched a new initiative to reach women and marginalized communities through investment in a tailored massive open online course (MOOC) platform, called Doroob.[17] In May 2015, the country signed a new agreement with UNESCO's International Bureau of Education to pursue a new education reform initiative focused, as in the UAE, on raising the quality of education.[18] Over the past 15 years, the country has also dramatically expanded access to higher education. According to Saudi officials, enrollment in universities doubled between 2003 and 2013, from around 750,000 students in 8 public and a handful of private universities to "over 1.2 million students in 5 public universities and 30 private universities and colleges."[19]

In interviews, several educators and education experts in Saudi Arabia attributed most of the problems with Saudi schools to the failure to reform the teaching corps and administration: the education sector was one of the first to be

[14] Samihah Zaman, "Curriculum Reforms to Develop Graduates for UAE Workforce," *Gulf News*, March 25, 2015, http://gulfnews.com/news/uae/education/curriculum-reform-to-develop-graduates-for-uae-workforce-1.1478845.
[15] Interviews, Dubai and Al Ain, November 2013.
[16] Interviews, Abu Dhabi and Dubai, November 2013; see also Alpen Capital, "GCC Education Industry," July 2, 2014, http://www.alpencapital.com/downloads/GCC_Education_Industry_Report_July_2014.pdf.
[17] "Saudi Arabia Approves $21 bln 5-Year Education Plan," Reuters, May 19, 2014, http://www.reuters.com/article/2014/05/19/saudi-education-idUSL6N0O53HU20140519; "Saudi Arabia and EdX Join Forces to Bridge the Gap," EdX, July 15, 2014, https://www.edx.org/press/saudi-arabia-edx-join-forces-bridge-gap. See also Doroob's website at https://www.doroob.sa/en/.
[18] International Bureau of Education, "IBE and the Ministry of Education of Saudi Arabia Sign Agreement on Quality and Excellence of Education," May 5, 2015, http://www.ibe.unesco.org/en/global-news-archive/single-news/news/ibe-and-the-ministry-of-education-of-saudi-arabia-sign-agreement-on-quality-and-excellence-of-educat.html.
[19] Dr. Ahmad Al-Jubaili, "Saudi Arabia—Dramatic Developments in Higher Education," *QS Showcase*, February 11, 2014, http://qsshowcase.com/main/saudi-arabia-dramatic-developments-in-higher-education/.

"Saudized" (raising the proportion of Saudis employed in place of expatriates) despite the lack of trained professionals, and many schools are now staffed by employees ill-equipped to implement reforms or improve quality.[20] Some who advocate expanding the country's private educational options argue that it is the only way to circumvent an essentially unreformable education system.[21]

Recent shake-ups after the death of King Abdullah in January of this year leave the future of Saudi Arabia's education system uncertain. Among King Salman's first decrees was the consolidation of the ministries of education and higher education into one new ministry, which could indicate a desire to facilitate future reforms. On the other hand, he removed the female deputy education minister from her post, and his new royal adviser is "a cleric whom King Abdullah had dismissed for criticizing the country's first coed university," the King Abdullah University for Science and Technology.[22] But other efforts continue on the sidelines. Saudi Aramco, the state oil company that is often tasked with devising and implementing projects in parallel with state institutions, has been working to create "centers of excellence" at Saudi schools, where teachers will study learner-centered teaching methods and ways to integrate technologies into their curricula. "Hopefully, the Ministry of Education will follow our lead," one Aramco official said.

> Even when educators get an opportunity to emphasize critical thinking, broader imperatives to instill national and culturally conservative values can hamper their efforts.

Other GCC countries have reforms under way too. Oman implemented major education reforms in the mid-1990s to strengthen STEM education and English, and it is currently developing a new strategy, the Oman Education Vision 2040, which will outline the path forward for its education sector.[23] Qatar implemented a dramatic reform of its public education system in the early 2000s, when a plan developed by U.S. policy researchers introduced independent schools to encourage innovation.[24] The government has also undertaken ambitious reforms in its higher education and research sectors, the results of which will be seen in the coming years.[25]

[20] Interviews, Al Khobar, Riyadh, and Jeddah, January 2014.
[21] Interview with a private school network director, Jeddah, January 2014.
[22] Ben Hubbard, "King Salman Upends Status Quo in Region and the Royal Family," New York Times, May 10, 2015, http://www.nytimes.com/2015/05/11/world/middleeast/king-salman-upends-status-quo-in-region-and-the-royal-family.html.
[23] "Oman Discusses National Education Strategy 2040," Oman News Agency, June 3, 2013, http://www.muscatdaily.com/Archive/Oman/Oman-discusses-National-Education-Strategy-2040-2b35. Other discussions have indicated that a new round of education reform, focused on strengthening vocational offerings, could appear soon. Maryam Khan, "Oman Planning to Revamp Its Education System as Part of Roadmap 2020," Muscat Daily, October 16, 2014, http://www.muscatdaily.com/Archive/Oman/Oman-planning-to-revamp-its-education-system-as-part-of-roadmap-2040-3it7.
[24] Qatar Ministry of Education, Education and Training Sector Strategy; Gail Zellman et al., Implementation of the K-12 Reforms in Qatar's Education System (Santa Monica: RAND-Qatar Policy Institute, 2009), http://www.rand.org/content/dam/rand/pubs/monographs/2009/RAND_MG880.pdf.

At times, political sensitivities or shifts have stood in the way of adopting or implementing education reforms. For example, Kuwait announced new education reforms in December 2013, but political gridlock means that these changes will likely be slow to materialize.[26] Bahrain launched a National Economic Strategy in 2009 and another for 2011–2014 that included major reforms to higher education, improvements to the K-12 school system, and development of occupational standards and training in line with the new Bahrain Qualifications Framework; but political developments in the country since 2011 have sidelined many of those reforms.[27]

Education reform is not only about improving school quality. One of the major goals of education reform across the region is to instill in students the values and character traits that will facilitate both their entry into the workforce and their loyalty to the political status quo. Policymakers in the UAE have increasingly focused their energy on education reform because they have concluded that shaping children's education is the best approach to shaping their character, work ethic, and career orientations—making them not only model workers, but also model citizens.[28] In accordance with these goals, they are trying to change the perception that teaching is an undesirable career and to recruit more Emiratis as teachers, because "Emirati students need Emirati teachers...for complex community and cultural reasons."[29] Qatar is also focusing on identity. Its national education strategy, which seeks to make Qatar a competitive knowledge-based economy, calls for "the strengthening of the national identity; the integration of national heritage, and Arab and Islamic values into all educational curricula and practices"—and even seeks to increase student participation in (approved) civil society organizations.[30]

Even when educators get an opportunity to emphasize critical thinking, broader imperatives to instill national and culturally conservative values can hamper their efforts. A recent study on the educational system in Kuwait, for example, found that the political and social aims of the educational system undermined its purported educational goals. The curriculum and teaching still promoted uncritical nationalism, rigid religious doctrine, and national unity and loyalty.[31] A relatively successful initiative to expand the curriculum in civics—teaching Kuwaiti students

[25] Alan S. Weber, "Linking Education to Creating a Knowledge Society: Qatar's Investment in the Education Sector," in *Handbook of Research on Higher Education in the MENA Region: Policy and Practice* (Hershey, PA: IGI Global, 2014), 52–73.
[26] "Kuwait Steps Up the Pace on Education Reform," Oxford Business Group, December 2013, http://www.oxfordbusinessgroup.com/economic_updates/kuwait-steps-pace-education-reform.
[27] Bahrain Economic Development Board, *Annual Report 2011*, http://www.bahrainedb.com/en/EDBDocuments/EDB%27s-Annual-Report-2011.pdf.
[28] Calvert W. Jones, "Bedouins into Bourgeois? Social Engineering for a Market Economy in the United Arab Emirates" (PhD dissertation, Yale University, 2013).
[29] "Emiratisation in Education Must Succeed," *National*, January 1, 2015, http://www.thenational.ae/opinion/editorial/emiratisation-in-education-must-succeed. The editorial notes that although ADEC has successfully increased its recruitment of nationals, most of them have gone into management or administrative roles, rather than into teaching.
[30] Qatar Ministry of Education, *Education and Training Sector Strategy*, 10.
[31] Rania al-Nakib, "Education and Democratic Development in Kuwait: Citizens in Waiting" (Chatham House Research Paper, London, March 2015), 3, http://www.chathamhouse.org/sites/files/chathamhouse/field/field_document/20150408Kuwait.pdf.

about the constitution, human rights, and democracy over the course of three years in high school—was scaled back in 2010 to a less effective one-year program.[32] That this occurred in Kuwait—the GCC country with the most developed experience of electoral institutions and democratic participation—suggests how difficult implementing systems that teach critical and innovative thinking may be across the rest of the region.

States have also pursued policies that seek to get students out of their home cultures and into foreign institutions. All GCC governments offer generous scholarships to help their most talented students pursue university and graduate education abroad. Some programs have been around for decades, and they usually emphasize studies in STEM disciplines.[33] More recently, Saudi Arabia has scaled this effort to a new level. The King Abdullah Scholarship Program, begun in 2005, has sent more than 150,000 young Saudis abroad to pursue higher education since 2005, at a cost of $2.4 billion annually; according to Saudi government data three-quarters of Saudis who study abroad now do so through KASP.[34]

Some Saudi liberals and foreign observers seem to hope that the initiative will inject more liberal values and culture into Saudi Arabia, or that it will undermine the role that conservatives play in the country's educational system.[35] It remains too soon to judge what the program's ultimate impact will be.

Career Education

Governments and other institutions are beginning to try to develop human capital through career education as well through traditional education. Across the region, the approach to presenting career options in schools remains fragmented and unstructured, and lacks coordination with the job market.[36] Many working in the region emphasize that youth need help conceptualizing from a young age what a "career" itself is—as opposed simply to a job—and what can make a career exciting. Schools in the region usually have little interaction with companies outside of the public and semipublic sector, and most national students come from families where people have traditionally held public sector jobs. As a result, young nationals often don't know what careers are available to them.[37]

> Across the region, the approach to presenting career options in schools remains fragmented and unstructured, and lacks coordination with the job market.

[32] Ibid., 14.

[33] The exact nature of these programs varies. Some require that the students return and work for the government after they complete their education, while others do not. They vary in the amount of money they provide students to cover living expenses, and some provide bonuses for strong academic performances.

[34] Charles Taylor and Wasmiah Albasri, "The Impact of Saudi Arabia King Abdullah's Scholarship Program in the U.S.," *Open Journal of Social Sciences* 2 (2014): 112–13.

[35] Ibid.; see also Stefanie A. Hausheer, "Not the Saudi Arabia You Hear About: The Students Abroad Factor," Saudi-US Relations Information Service, February 26, 2014, http://susris.com/2014/02/26/not-the-saudi-arabia-you-hear-about-the-students-abroad-factor-hausheer/.

[36] Multiple interviews in the UAE and Saudi Arabia, November 2013–January 2014.

[37] World Economic Forum, *Rethinking Arab Unemployment* (Geneva: World Economic Forum, 2014), 11.

Some new programs try to expose young people to work environments before they reach the point of needing a job. Many young people finishing school and entering the workforce in the Gulf have no work experience whatsoever, whether from part-time, volunteer, or internship experiences. According to a recent poll, between 32 percent (UAE) and 43 percent of youth (Oman, Saudi Arabia, and Kuwait) in GCC countries had no work experience prior to or during college and university. Of those who had worked, between 37 percent (Qatar) and 68 percent (Oman) had 6 months' experience or less.[38] Career education efforts that do exist assume that changing the experiences and opportunities young people have while they are in school is central to changing their ambitions. For example, the UAE's Absher Initiative runs a program for teenagers called "Yes to Work" that combines classroom instruction and on-the-job experience in retail environments; the program seeks both "to show Emirati students how important it [work] is to the country so that they are able to fill roles typically occupied by expatriates" and to show employers that Emirati youth are ready to work.[39] In Saudi Arabia, the women's college Effat University in Jeddah requires most students to undertake an internship before they graduate. The college often has to work to convince employers to accept female interns in the first place, but administrators there report that after working with the college's students, many of the employers want to hire them and to bring on more interns. In the process, the college sees itself not only giving young women new opportunities, but helping to change perceptions of Saudi women as prospective employees in the Saudi private sector.[40]

But policymakers are also increasingly focused on interventions through which they can target young people who have already finished school and are seeking to enter the job market. The Saudi Ministry of Labor, for instance, has implemented career education and development programs, including Project Parallel, which teaches employability skills, and it also offers short courses and has established job placement centers.[41] The ministry is working to develop "a comprehensive career education and development system" for the country that would reach into K-12 schools, and its MOOC platform Doroob represents a major initiative to expand Saudis' access to training and educational opportunities outside of the traditional school system.[42] Private sector companies in Saudi Arabia are also working to expand career education in and out of schools, including by establishing regular job fairs that reach thousands of students.[43]

[38] Bayt.com and YouGov, "Work Experience Acquired Prior to or During College/University," YouGov/Bayt.com Fresh Graduates in the MENA Survey, July 2014, 50, http://img.b8cdn.com/images/uploads/article_docs/bayt-fresh-grad_-july-2014_21182_EN.pdf.

[39] Hareth Al Bustani, "Emirati Teenagers Say Yes to Work Placements," National, August 6, 2014, http://www.thenational.ae/uae/education/emirati-teenagers-say-yes-to-work-placements.

[40] Interviews, Jeddah, January 2014.

[41] G20, "Employment Plan 2014: Saudi Arabia," https://g20.org/wp-content/uploads/2014/12/g20_employment_plan_saudi_arabia.pdf.

[42] Ibid., phone interview with Saudi Ministry of Labor staff, March 2014.

[43] Interview with a private sector corporate social responsibility (CSR) officer, Al Khobar, January 2014.

These programs sometimes touch on sensitive social issues. One career fair for girls in Saudi Arabia, for example, provoked pushback from parents when it featured filmmaking as a possible career for women.[44] Nonetheless, one of the most successful developments in recent years has been the establishment of career fairs and forums geared specifically toward women. Glowork, the leader in this field, has placed more than 10,000 women in jobs and is now working closely with the Ministry of Labor.[45] Other approaches are being piloted, too. In Riyadh, the King Khalid Foundation is working with the International Youth Foundation to implement a pilot of its Passport to Success program, which helps young people examine their values and interests and identify career goals.[46] Cultural programming—such as Saudi Aramco's traveling educational exhibition iThra—also aims to promote reading, critical thinking, knowledge of science, and awareness of diverse career fields among young people.[47]

Education and employment policymakers in the UAE are also expanding the depth and range of career guidance available to students, particularly Emiratis. In the past, the government has relied primarily on personal connections, large job fairs (such as the annual and ongoing Careers UAE exposition), and government-run job placement programs to channel nationals into public sector careers.[48] Leaders in education and youth empowerment organizations in both Abu Dhabi and Dubai talk about the need to better educate students about their options so that they choose "disciplines which have jobs" or consider unconventional career paths.[49] In March 2015, ADEC launched the first formal, comprehensive career guidance system at the university level for the emirate of Abu Dhabi, which will aim to help students evaluate their own goals and guide them toward appropriate study and career choices—particularly in STEM disciplines—as part of an effort "to empower higher education students to take control of their future."[50] In July 2015, a revision to the UAE's labor law noted plans to introduce a new National Employment Section at the Ministry of Labor, which would shoulder primary responsibility for finding nationals employment and helping companies identify nationals to hire.[51]

[44] Ibid.

[45] Interview with Glowork leaders, Riyadh, January 2014.

[46] Interview with King Khalid Foundation staff, Riyadh, January 2014.

[47] Interviews with Saudi Aramco staff, Dhahran, January 2014.

[48] The Abu Dhabi Tawteen Council was tasked with finding job placements—any job placement—for unemployed Emiratis, but some claimed it offered little more than a portal to apply for jobs, and the organization was overhauled in late 2014. Ayesha Al Khoori, "Emirati Graduates Unhappy with Recruitment Procedures," *National*, August 5, 2014, http://www.thenational.ae/uae/emirati-graduates-unhappy-with-recruitment-procedures; "Board of Abu Dhabi Tawteen Council Restructured," Emirates News Agency, August 26, 2014, http://www.wam.ae/en/news/emirates/1395268952935.html. On Careers UAE see "Maktoum Opens Careers UAE 2015," *Emirates247*, April 28, 2015, http://www.emirates247.com/news/government/maktoum-opens-careers-uae-2015-2015-04-28-1.588919.

[49] Interviews, Abu Dhabi, Dubai, and Ras al-Khaimah, November 2013; Muaz Shahbandri, "Getting Emiratis into Private Sector a Challenge, Says Education Expert," *Khaleej Times*, December 12, 2014, http://www.khaleejtimes.com/article/20141211/ARTICLE/312119966/1014.

[50] Abu Dhabi Education Council, "ADEC Introduces the First Higher Education Career Guidance System in Abu Dhabi," March 24, 2015, https://www.adec.ac.ae/en/mediacenter/news/pages/adec-introduces-the-first-higher-education.aspx.

[51] Martin Fullard, "UAE Labour Law: Employing a Worker in the UAE," *Gulf News*, July 1, 2015, http://gulfnews.com/guides/life/law-finance/uae-labour-law-employing-a-worker-in-the-uae-1.1542972.

Successful vocational training programs and structured internship opportunities remain the exception rather than the norm across the Gulf, but they are expanding. GCC governments have invested in technical and vocational education and training (TVET), though such programs do not yet reach many people. The appeal of these programs has suffered from both structural economic factors (better-paying jobs are still not that hard to get) and social prejudice (few want the low-paying jobs for which TVET would prepare them). In addition, it is relatively easy for most GCC nationals to attend a nonvocational educational institution.[52] In Saudi Arabia, upward of 90 percent of high school graduates attend university; in the UAE, the figure is comparable for women, though only about 50 percent of male graduates continue to university.[53] One Emirati policymaker noted that expanding vocational education will be a significant point of focus over the next 5 to 10 years—but that the government will have to first change mind-sets toward different kinds of work and education in order for it to be a success.

Some initiatives partner private companies with educational institutions to provide internship opportunities or to help develop vocational or training programs that lead directly to jobs. For example, Saudi Arabia's Technical and Vocational Training Corporation (TVTC) has spearheaded partnerships with foreign companies to establish and run technical and vocational schools in specific areas (such as automobile maintenance) that feed into employment opportunities with the foreign company.[54] At one such institute, the Higher Institute for Plastics Fabrication in Riyadh, Japanese firms developed the curriculum and conduct yearly audits to ensure the quality of instruction is meeting international standards.[55] The TVTC recently announced a dramatic planned expansion of the technical and vocational sector in Saudi Arabia, and it has signed partnerships with 33 private sector companies to establish training institutes. The plan aims to triple the number of trainees by 2020, from current levels of around 110,000 to 300,000.[56] Private education providers have taken note of the government's strong interest in TVET, too, and see its growth as a business opportunity.[57]

In the UAE, emirate-level institutions (such as the Abu Dhabi Centre for Technical and Vocational Education and Training [ACTVET] and the KHDA in Dubai) promote technical training and vocational education. But progress on actually building

[52] According to one administrator at a community college in Saudi Arabia, one of the greatest challenges in attracting Saudi students is that it is so easy for them to be accepted into a four-year university, even if they are unprepared.
[53] Interviews, Abu Dhabi and Riyadh, November 2013 and January 2014. See also Ridge, *Education and the Reverse Gender Divide in the Gulf States*.
[54] See the TVTC website at http://www.tvtc.gov.sa.
[55] Interview with HIFP staff, Riyadh, January 2014.
[56] M. D. Al-Sulami, "TVTC Ties Up with Private Partners for Training," *Arab News*, January 11, 2015, http://www.arabnews.com/saudi-arabia/news/687756.
[57] Alpen Capital, "GCC Education Industry."

such programs is embryonic at best. Qatar has outlined ambitious goals to advance a TVET sector in its 2011–2016 development strategy—placing great emphasis on "changing perceptions" of vocational education—but the strategy's focus on the basics highlights how underdeveloped the sector is to date.[58] In Kuwait, the Public Authority for Applied Education and Training (PAAET), founded in 1982, serves as an umbrella organization overseeing both vocational education initiatives and broader education reform. Yet even today, vocational education is undervalued, underdemanded, and poorly understood in Kuwait.[59] In Bahrain, TVET institutes have existed for decades,[60] but enrollment in TVET programs as a proportion of all secondary school enrollments actually declined from 2000 to 2012,[61] and in March 2014, Labor Ministry Undersecretary Sabah Salem Al-Dosary lamented TVET's "slow growth" in Bahrain.[62] In Oman, TVET was introduced in the 1970s and has regularly expanded,[63] but a recent study found that the system's graduates fail to acquire skills that actually help them get jobs in the Omani private sector.[64]

Promoting Entrepreneurship

The trendiest component of human capital development—and specifically of efforts to broaden the range of occupations which Gulf citizens take up—is programs that promote or fund entrepreneurship. These include start-up incubators, business competitions, initiatives to provide seed funding for small and medium-size enterprises, and entrepreneurship clubs or programming in schools.

Public and private institutions in this field include N2V, Badir, Wa'ed, Sirb, ArabNeurs, Endeavor Saudi Arabia, and the KAUST New Ventures Seed Fund in Saudi Arabia; Tenmou and Tamkeen in Bahrain; SeedStartup, TwoFour54, Afkar, the Dubai Silicon Oasis Authority, in5, Turn8, and i360accelerator in the UAE; the Qatar Business Incubation Centre in Qatar; and myriad others in a rapidly evolving field.[65] Many of these new initiatives focus on tech start-ups and innovation, but others explicitly promote all kinds of small and medium-size enterprises.[66] The new Emirates Award for the Arabian Gulf Youth, for example, explicitly seeks to support social entrepreneurship

[58] Qatar Ministry of Education, *Qatar Education and Training Sector Strategy*, 22.

[59] Wendy Bilboe, "Vocational Education and Training in Kuwait: Vocational Education versus Values and Viewpoints," *International Journal of Training Research* 9 (2011): 256–60; see also the PAAET's website at http://tvetpaaet.com/en/about-paaet/. There seem to be some efforts to inject greater capacity into the sector. In mid-2014, Kuwait hosted its first Conference of Technical Vocational Training & Education to raise the profile of the PAAET.

[60] Ministry of Foreign Affairs of the Kingdom of Bahrain, "Bahrain's Education System," http://www.mofa.gov.bh/Default.aspx?tabid=7741.

[61] UNESCO, "Education for All Global Monitoring Report, Regional Overview: Arab States" (2015), 4, https://en.unesco.org/gem-report/sites/gem-report/files/regional_overview_AS_en.pdf.

[62] "Bahraini Vocational Education and Training Experience Highlighted," Bahrain News Agency, March 30, 2014, http://www.bna.bh/portal/en/news/611257.

[63] Technological Vocational Education and Training Oman, "TVET-Oman: About," http://www.tvetoman.net/Pages.php?PiD=2.

[64] Maimoona Al Rawahi and Vian Ahmed, "Factors Influencing the Effective Implementation of VET in Government Vocational Training Centres in Oman," CIB 2014 International Conference Proceedings, http://www.cib2014.org/proceedings/files/papers/680.pdf.

[65] These represent a mix of public and private initiatives. In the UAE, for example, the Dubai Silicon Oasis Authority is an initiative of the government of Dubai; Turn8 was created by DP World (a semipublic company that owns and manages the Jebel Ali sea terminal in Dubai and dozens of other ports); and SeedStartup is a wholly private initiative.

across the region.[67] GCC policymakers routinely celebrate and promote the idea that youth should embrace entrepreneurship, and the UAE has declared 2015 the "Year of Innovation."

Developments in the region's entrepreneurship scene are uneven and often difficult to judge because many of them are so new. The UAE leads other GCC countries in terms of the sophistication and extent of its entrepreneurship ecosystem. Yet structural barriers to success for new businesses—discussed further below—and the state origins of much of the funding for business development threaten to make entrepreneurship promotion an exercise in patronage rather than an engine of real economic growth. Recent research by Wamda, a regionally based organization providing media coverage and analysis of entrepreneurship in the Middle East, shows that new businesses across the region face significant challenges in acquiring funding and scaling their business models.[68] Other entrepreneurs, educators, and business professionals in the Gulf noted that in the absence of an innovative basic science and technology research sector in the GCC, many local start-ups and businesses focus primarily on adapting innovations developed elsewhere and applying them in the Gulf context.[69] It also remains the case that a small number of individuals pursue entrepreneurial career paths.

Challenging Cultures
GCC states have thus invested heavily in helping their people learn and succeed, and they have set lofty strategic goals for establishing knowledge-based economies. They have high expectations for the outcomes of these efforts. Although many efforts are nascent or have not yet had a big impact, they have nonetheless contributed to some social changes.

Many young people in the Gulf have taken full advantage of the investments made in their talent and capacity. Those who excel are given unparalleled resources and are globally competitive leaders and professionals. They are highly visible within their own societies and in interactions with people from other countries. They are entrepreneurial and pragmatic, speak excellent English, and know how to interact across cultures. Many of these individuals are deeply grateful for the opportunities they have been granted, aware of their good fortune, and eager to give back to their countries. They are also in high demand: according to one recruiter at a semi-private company in the UAE, the various companies and orga-

For a more detailed discussion of the start-up scene in the Middle East more broadly, see Christopher Schroeder, *Startup Rising: The Entrepreneurial Revolution Remaking the Middle East* (New York: Palgrave Macmillan, 2013); see also the Wamda website at http://www.wamda.com/.
See the Emirates Award for the Arabian Gulf Youth website at http://eaagy.emiratesfoundation.ae/awards.aspx.
Jamil Wyne and Estee Ward, "Enhancing Access: Assessing the Funding Landscape for MENA's Startups," Wamda Research Lab, October 2014, https://s3-eu-west-1.amazonaws.com/wrl-reports/english/wrl-enhancing-access.pdf; Jamil Wyne, "The Next Step: Breaking Barriers to Scale for MENA's Entrepreneurs," Wamda Research Lab, March 2014, https://s3-eu-west-1.amazonaws.com/wrl-reports/english/wrl-nextstep-for-scale.pdf.
Multiple interviews, UAE and Saudi Arabia, November 2013–January 2014.

nizations that are part of the "real knowledge economy" in the country compete fiercely with one another and the government for the most talented Emiratis.

In interviews with the author, a wide range of interlocutors across education, government, and the private sector in both the UAE and Saudi Arabia talked about dramatic generational shifts they are seeing. They made the following observations, among others:

- Young people are more educated and aware of how to succeed than in the past.

- Young people are more individualistic than in the past.

- Young people are more entrepreneurial and outward-looking than in the past.

- Young people need to feel they can make a difference through their work.

- More and more young people find the traditional path of public sector employment boring.
  - They want more excitement, challenges, and diverse experiences.
  - They do not want to stay in one secure job.

- Women in particular are embracing new opportunities and pushing themselves to achieve academically, and they want something more challenging outside of school, too.

- People living in remote areas are often more engaged with their work than those in the cities and are hungry for opportunities to work.

But these changes are far from universal. Other Saudis argued that younger generations have a greater sense of entitlement than their predecessors, because they have never known what their countries were like before oil. And most acknowledged that the shifts described above are happening for a small percentage of the population; the majority, they say, "want government jobs, fear the private sector, and just want security," as a Saudi educator put it. Another Saudi suggested that the motivation and competitiveness on display among elite performers represented "competition within elite families" for social status amid cosmopolitan norms more than widespread social change.

While it remains for future research to tease out in greater detail how prevalent each set of attitudes is, there are clearly multiple simultaneous responses to efforts to develop human capital. Frustrations among the ambitious, reinforcement of entitlement mind-sets, and widespread apathy and disengagement coexist in Gulf societies and, and each has different social and political implications.

Fostering Frustration

In the process of creating greater opportunities and capabilities for citizens, governments also raise citizens' ambitions and expectations, which may then be disappointed. For those who embrace the very entrepreneurial, solution-oriented mind-set that policymakers say they desire (whether as actual entrepreneurs or simply as go-getters within the bureaucracy or the private sector), obstacles in their path—in their own societies, in their interactions with expatriates, and in their own governments—may seem especially grating.

Cultural norms or restrictions may be one source of frustration for this group. These vary widely across the GCC, and are of particular importance as they relate to the roles and ambitions of women. A range of educators and employers interviewed in the UAE and Saudi Arabia saw women as more capable and more motivated than their male peers, and as a reason to be optimistic about the region's economic future.[70] This view was especially prevalent in the UAE, where educators and employers repeatedly praised women's drive and aptitude and cited them as top performers. But while many women have built very impressive careers, many others still face informal barriers. Across the region, women tend to have higher educational attainment rates than their male counterparts—sometimes to a dramatic degree—yet their labor force participation remains much lower. Even among those who seek jobs, unemployment rates for women are far higher.[71] Many workplaces across the region are integrated (though not in Saudi Arabia) and most people are comfortable with that integration,[72] but social pressures to be home by a certain hour, care for children, not travel far away, or avoid professions seen as "male" still hold women back. How parents (particularly fathers) feel about their daughters working also plays a large role in their workforce participation.[73] In fact, women's high rates of pursuing graduate education are in part a response to social obstacles to working—one educator in the UAE noted that going to graduate school "solves women's issues," so many of them leap at the chance. Many women are also interested in part-time work as a path forward; according to the director of Glowork, a majority of Saudi women the company surveyed were interested in having a part-time job.[74] In Saudi Arabia, where gender segregation remains rigid, the government has advanced initiatives in recent years that aim to help women work while avoiding gender mixing. These include efforts to get more Saudi women hired in the retail sector (where they serve other women) and promoting telework options, which allow women to work from home or from women-only call centers.

In Saudi Arabia, the ambitions of an educated generation of both men and women sometimes clash starkly with conservative social and religious norms. Officials at Saudi Aramco, for example, spoke of their desire to "Aramco-ize"

[70] In a recent book on the gender divide in Gulf education, Natasha Ridge argues that such comments do not adequately explain the relative underachievement of men—whose perceived apathy, laziness, or poor ability can be better ascribed to their treatment within the educational system. Ridge, *Education and the Reverse Gender Divide in the Gulf States*.

[71] Ibid. Ridge provides an extended discussion of this topic.

[72] With the exception of Saudi Arabia, more than two-thirds of surveyed women worked in a mixed workplace, with on average less than 10 percent of respondents in each GCC country reporting that they felt uncomfortable in that environment. Most (more than 50 percent in all GCC countries, up to 85 percent in some) felt comfortable or extremely comfortable in that environment. Bayt.com and YouGov, The Bayt.com Status of Women Working in the Middle East Survey, November 2014, 3. http://img.b8cdn.com/images/uploads/article_docs/bayt_women_workplace_2014_final_23102_EN.pdf.

[73] Emilie Rutledge, Mohamed Madi, and Ingo Forstenlechner, "Parental Influence on Female Vocational Decisions in the Arabian Gulf" (MPRA Paper No. 47521, June 13, 2014), http://mpra.ub.uni-muenchen.de/47521/1/MPRA_paper_47521.pdf.

[74] Interview with Glowork director, Riyadh, January 2014.

Saudi society by instilling values like excellence, professionalism, work ethic, and tolerance in the young people they work with and in the educational system more broadly. But they are also very conscious that in a country where the government bills itself as a guarantor of a particular vision of Islamic morality, any suggestion that current values are at fault may face pushback. Conservative social actors may criticize initiatives to promote entrepreneurship, employ more women, spur creative thinking, or get young people into new fields as efforts to "Westernize" society, even though, as many GCC nationals themselves point out, there is no incompatibility between Islam and such values.

Entrepreneurs run into some of the biggest frustrations. Many young people in the region—approximately three-quarters in one survey—would rather own a business than be an employee,[75] and the public and private promotion of entrepreneurship in the region has expanded interest in finding ways to start new businesses. Yet those wishing to become entrepreneurs face significant structural obstacles.[76] Regulatory systems, including the lack of bankruptcy laws, can make the consequences of failure dire in some economic ventures. Many said that ecosystems for entrepreneurship in the Gulf

> In Saudi Arabia, the ambitions of an educated generation of both men and women sometimes clash starkly with conservative social and religious norms.

remain fundamentally unsupportive to those eager to start a new business, despite the high-profile technology and innovation programs and start-up incubators.[77] Patronage and corruption in various economic sectors deter innovation and keep entrepreneurs from entering closed markets. One Saudi entrepreneur said, for example, that his first business failed not because the model was unviable, but because he had not realized that an important family controlled the industry he was trying to break into. Other Saudis and Emiratis reiterated that most successful entrepreneurs have families with government and business connections, and that historical patterns of patronage are shaping how new businesses emerge today. Young people are acutely aware of the barriers they face, and can be deterred by them.

But barriers to being entrepreneurial are also cultural. Around the world, successful entrepreneurs often reject established paths and structures. They learn to try and fail, and they are allowed to do so. Many argued that fear of or aversion to failure has cultural roots in the Gulf in the importance of family and tribal honor—and the taboo of shame—as well as in privilege. A private sector executive observing the entrepreneurship scene in the UAE said

[75] Bayt.com, Millennials in the Middle East and North Africa Survey, February 10, 2014, http://www.bayt.com/en/research-report-19564/.
[76] Wyne, "The Next Step"; World Economic Forum, Rethinking Arab Unemployment, 11.
[77] Most recently, Qatar recent launched a Business Incubation Center (worth $27.4 million) to "give a boost to entrepreneurship in the country," as part of its Qatar National Vision 2030 initiatives. "Incubation Centre Aims to Give Qatar Start-ups a Boost," Gulf Times, September 14, 2014, http://www.gulf-times.com/qatar/178/details/408169/incubation-centre-aims-to-give-qatar-start-ups-a-boost.

that institutions acknowledged the need for entrepreneurship, but noted that "it doesn't work if failures remain a huge roadblock [to personal success]." And a Saudi entrepreneur observed, "It's possible to teach people the concept of 'fail fast,' but then negative community attitudes override people's inspiration." Families often discourage plans to forgo a stable job opportunity to try something new. Workplace cultures may also discourage entrepreneurial behavior. One young Emirati man in Dubai described the difference between his private sector job, where he felt challenged and empowered to suggest new ideas, and the government job he took some years later, where he felt utterly stifled by the bureaucracy and lack of openness to suggestions from below. Frustration in bureaucratic environments is hardly unique to the UAE or the Gulf, but it is especially consequential in an environment where so many people work in bureaucracies and the most talented are frequently groomed for government work.

If they do go into the private sector, nationals may become frustrated that their ability to contribute goes unrecognized. Other research has noted that nationals in the private sector "perceive a degree of 'tokenism'" and have the sense that "I am here to fill a job, and my employer isn't really interested in my long-term progression and advancement."[78] Employers also generally hold lower expectations of nationals.[79] Many young people feel that abilities and attitudes toward work have shifted markedly in the past decade or so, but also believe that private companies have held onto past prejudices about Gulf nationals not being good workers. The imposition of quotas through Saudization or Emiratization schemes can make this dynamic worse—companies may feel that since they have to hire nationals, they may do so without the genuine intention to invest in and utilize those employees' skills. That creates a negative feedback loop where employers (who are often foreign) resent nationals and nationals resent employers—and may end up "feeling lost in their own culture."[80]

Ambitious individuals also grow frustrated with political structures that limit their ability to influence the policies that shape their opportunities. Even basic policymaking processes, including decisions about spending on social services, are highly opaque. Public consultation on matters of government policy is limited to a circumscribed set of individuals viewed as experts and possessing the necessary social stature to influence decisionmakers. Even technocrats hired to produce policy recommendations report that the way to make their recommendations heard is to find a way to reach top decisionmakers directly. There is a clear hunger among youth to feel a connection to their policymakers and to have their voices and concerns heard. In a series of workshops and discussions between youth and Saudi officials organized by the King Khalid Foundation in 2012, participants repeatedly indicated that they wanted those in power to understand their struggles and that they wanted more communication with

[78] David B. Jones and Radhika Punshi, *Unlocking the Paradox of Plenty* (Dubai: Motivate Publishing, 2013), 38.
[79] Ibid.
[80] "UAE Strives to Engage the Young, Gifted, but Bored," BBC, April 6, 2015, http://www.bbc.com/news/world-middle-east-31986652.

policymakers.[81] These comments do not necessarily mean that youth desire a radical change to systems and forms of governance. It does mean that they want to feel they have a stake in the system that already exists.

In Saudi Arabia in particular, these kinds of frustrations, combined with the government's emphasis on providing students with educational opportunities abroad, could lead to brain drain. It is not yet clear whether the tens of thousands of students who head out on KASP scholarships want to return or seek to stay abroad. Anecdotally, Saudis report having heard that young women being educated abroad increasingly want to stay abroad and work. Because of the financial safety net they enjoy, young Saudis are unlikely ever to seek to migrate abroad in as great numbers as their counterparts in North Africa; but a choice by the most talented and ambitious to stay away from the country would represent a significant lost investment for the government—and a loss of talent that could drive further change in the Saudi economy and society.

Reinforcing Privilege and Patronage

Another outcome of efforts to develop human capital is the reinforcement of feelings of entitlement and privilege. In trying to find ways to get citizens to go against the grain of economic incentives and embrace private sector work—by offering subsidies, special programs, and awards, or encouraging employers to do the same—governments and companies raise expectations about the kind of treatment nationals can expect to receive in school and the workplace in perpetuity.

Overcoming the incentives to accept public sector work requires offering workarounds and alternatives.[82] In addition to setting quotas for how many nationals companies must hire (or are strongly encouraged to hire), governments may require that companies provide benefits or accommodations for nationals that they need not provide their other employees. Private companies may also decide that they ought to provide special benefits to attract and retain nationals for reputational reasons.[83] These efforts to boost private sector employment through subsidies or perks send a message that nationals always deserve or require an extra helping hand, and that they represent a privileged economic, as well as political, class within their countries.

This is the case even though both private and public institutions acknowledge that new national employees require significant training. Human resource professionals in both the UAE and Saudi Arabia discussed needing training initiatives spanning two to three years that cover

[81] Workshop summary shared with the author, King Khalid Foundation, 2012; see also Kristin Diwan Smith, "The Contest for 'Youth' in the GCC," POMEPS, March 21, 2014. http://pomeps.org/2014/03/21/the-contest-for-youth-in-the-gcc/.
[82] For a good discussion of these incentives and the various policies debated to overcome or accommodate them, see Hertog, Arab Gulf States: An Assessment.
[83] Academic research on this subject supports the idea that foreign firms, at least, can improve their reputation and connections by hiring locals in the Gulf. Ingo Forstenlechner and Kamel Mellahib, "Gaining Legitimacy through Hiring Local Workforce at a Premium: The Case of MNEs in the United Arab Emirates," Journal of World Business 46, no. 4 (2011): 455–61. In interviews, several private sector executives suggested that bolstering local reputation is a primary reason for making a good-faith effort to hire nationals.

basic workplace skills and ethics. Though such programs usually address real skill deficits, managers also noted that most young employees see training opportunities as a reward and a break from work rather than as a way to improve their performance. "They want cash, and they want the job title," one manager said. At one privately-run bank in the UAE, a manager explained that all national employees must take a six-month remedial training course in math and English and well as customer service and other basic workplace skills. This training notwithstanding, the bank would not employ nationals as bank tellers—doing so was considered too risky, given that most saw direct customer service work as beneath them.

In the UAE, nationals are also encouraged to think of themselves as natural leaders and achievers by virtue of their nationality, and employers appeal to workers' pride in their identity in order to engage them. Interviewees in the UAE emphasized that in the government and the semiprivate sector, patriotism and national identity can be a strong motivator for Emirati workers. In the private sector, observers noted that representing the UAE and the Arab world internationally, working at a world-class company, and contributing to the UAE's global profile all appeal to young Emiratis' cosmopolitan aspirations and pride. Yet appeals to national identity might in effect reinforce a sense of entitlement to managerial positions. Emiratis who have been taught that their privilege entails a responsibility to lead could conclude that they must always be leaders. One scholar noted a comparable issue in the educational system, where Emirati students are constantly praised by expatriate teachers who feel pressure not to judge these students honestly. Students may then develop an attitude of "super-entitlement"[84]—expectations of constant success and praise—that can undermine the propensity for risk taking and innovation that policymakers hope to promote.

Saudi Arabia suffers from a different problem—the absence of an effort by the government to "ask youth to live the challenges of the country," as one entrepreneur put it. The sense of complacency and entitlement among youth is made worse, he argued, by a political system that has done little to communicate that the future will be different. According to one Saudi policymaker working on employment issues, the idea that Saudis cannot or will not accept real work is a myth, but it is true that "the younger generation are shocked that there are no jobs, and they can't get what others had before." That shock spurs some to pursue new paths, but merely angers others, who feel they are being denied opportunities that they see as their right.

In the entrepreneurship sphere, one concern is that absent the appropriate underlying ecosystem, support for entrepreneurship could merely reinforce expectations that the government will guarantee jobs and income. Much of the support for entrepreneurship in the GCC has been a top-down effort that cre-

Jones, "Bedouins into Bourgeois."
"None of it is bottom-up," said one individual who works with Saudi start-ups.

ates demand for funding and support rather than meeting a need for them.[85] One entrepreneur active in Saudi Arabia complained that government funds intended to foster start-up culture instead often went to wealthy young people who set up traditional service businesses (like beauty salons) and then hired expatriate workers to staff them. At a workshop in 2013, entrepreneurs in Bahrain complained that the state institution supporting small and medium enterprises, Tamkeen, handed out loans too easily, resulting in a proliferation of unneeded abaya and cupcake stores.[86] In the UAE, as well, a number of people noted a similar dynamic, in which funds for entrepreneurship or business plan competitions were in danger of becoming just another form of payout from the state unrelated to the promise, success, or failure of an initiative. One observer of this field argued that promoting entrepreneurship might work very well in the UAE in a few more years, after planned reforms to facilitate the creation of new businesses are implemented, but competitions for funding would still require oversight to ensure they were genuinely rigorous and not merely a new venue for handing out easy money.

Neglecting the Disengaged

Both frustration and a sense of entitlement coexist with complacency, apathy, and disengagement. While some may excel but grow frustrated, others get left behind. Guaranteed employment from which it is nearly impossible to be fired does not spur creativity or dedication (althought both may exist); the unmotivated easily grow disengaged when making money is not an urgent problem.

In any society, there are always some people who need a generous safety net, and several of the GCC countries have programs and policies that explicitly address the needs of marginalized groups. Some, for example, have implemented programs to incentivize hiring the disabled, including by allowing them to count in nationalization schemes as more than one employee.[87]

But conversations across the UAE and Saudi Arabia also suggested that policymakers, educators, and planners often informally write off certain subgroups—which together make up a majority of the population—as unlikely to ever contribute productively to the knowledge economy: these include women who, for social reasons, have difficulty breaking into the workforce; older workers who have trouble adjusting to new environments after years of holding jobs where little was expected of them; and people from marginalized groups in society. Discrimination, little discussed or studied, seems to affect outcomes. One private sector employer in the UAE spoke of candidates who lack access to the most engaging opportunities because they are from "the wrong family or the wrong emirate," and many Saudis spoke of tribe and city origin mattering significantly for the jobs to which young people had access. The perception that

[86] Nina Curley, "Not Another Cupcake Shop: Bahrain's Women Entrepreneurs Debate What Local Startups Need," Wamda, October 10, 2013, http://www.wamda.com/2013/10/not-another-cupcake-shop-bahrain-s-women-entrepreneurs-debate-what-local-startups-need.
[87] This is the case in Saudi Arabia, where each disabled employee counts as four Saudi employees in calculations of Saudization targets. Jennifer Peck, "Can Hiring Quotas Work? The Effect of the Nitaqat Program on the Saudi Private Sector" (Massachusetts Institute of Technology, Cambridge, MA, April 2014), 10, http://economics.mit.edu/files/9417.

older workers cannot be productive also came across strongly. In Saudi Arabia, one educator said that he believed that any government funds spent on people over the age of 30 were "wasted" funds, and that he had "given up hope" that those people would ever behave differently in the labor market. Experts on human capital and employment in the UAE expressed similar opinions.

High school dropouts and college underachievers also pose an especially vexing challenge for policymakers,[88] made all the more difficult by the gender imbalance in this group. Up to 25 percent of young Emirati men never finish high school, and across the GCC, men underperform women at university.[89] Addressing this "reverse gender gap" is especially challenging because people in positions of leadership tend "to focus on the increasing numbers of women persisting in their education and doing well at school."[90] More generally, in their understandable urge to celebrate human capital development successes, Gulf governments often gloss over the policy implications of having large groups of people who have not benefited from or taken advantage of their investments. One university educator said that discussions about how to promote resilience among Emirati students were premature; "Many of them do not care if they fail," she said. "For 50 percent of students, you first need to figure out how to motivate them to try in the first place." A policymaker working on employment in the UAE emphasized that many students still focus on obtaining the easiest degree possible that will credential them to seek a public sector job.

For all the success human capital schemes have had educating and empowering a talented elite, it is the average performers, neglected and floundering, who are most likely to depend on government employment or welfare and to pose challenges for policymakers in the future. One study found that in contrast to a common phenomenon in which radical Islamists are often recruited from among the educated (especially engineers), in Saudi Arabia this was not the case—top performers were generally snapped up into promising careers and engineers were not over-represented among radicals.[91] Other scholars have noted that "badly educated and unemployable Saudis," meanwhile, are attractive targets for radical recruitment.[92] Further investigation should seek to confirm what appears to be the case—that youth drawn into violent extremist

[88] Fatma Al-Marri and Mike Helal, *Addressing the Early School Leaving Challenge 2011* (Dubai: Knowledge and Human Development Authority, 2011), 14, https://www.khda.gov.ae/CMS/WebParts/TextEditor/Documents/Early_School_Leaving_Challenge_En.pdf. Note, however, that new figures in 2015 indicate that this trend is not necessarily permanent, and girls made up the majority of early school leavers in 2014. Nadeem Hanif, "More than 1,600 Pupils Drop Out from UAE Schools," *National*, January 4, 2015, http://www.thenational.ae/uae/education/more-than-1600-pupils-drop-out-from-uae-schools.

[89] Sara Hamdan, "In the Gulf, Boys Falling Behind in School," New York Times, May 27, 2012, http://www.nytimes.com/2012/05/28/world/middleeast/28iht-educlede28.html?_r=0.

[90] Ridge, *Education and the Reverse Gender Divide in the Gulf States*, 82.

[91] Diego Gambetta and Steffen Hertog, "Why are there so many Engineers among Islamic Radicals?" *European Journal of Sociology* 50, No. 2 (August 2009): 201–30, http://journals.cambridge.org/abstract_S0003975609990129.

[92] Caroline Montagu, "Civil Society in Saudi Arabia: The Power and Challenges of Association," Chatham House, March 2015, http://www.chathamhouse.org/sites/files/chathamhouse/field/field_document/20150331CivilSocietySaudiMontagu.pdf.

activity in this context are recruited from among the alienated and disengaged rather than from the high-performing, talented elite. More generally, under-achievement and disengagement have social consequences: both globally and in the Gulf, leaving school early is associated with worse health outcomes, lower earnings, and higher propensity to commit crime.[93]

Elites are both sympathetic to these disengaged youth and critical of them. One Saudi employment expert said it was "unfair" to hold youth entirely accountable for their situation—"we brainwashed them"—but he added, "it is also their responsibility to grow up." Others noted that part of the challenge lies in revising underlying social expectations about what makes a person worthy of respect. As a Saudi private sector employer explained, "Here, a person's value comes from his tribe and the number of children he has, not from his accomplishments or efficiency." Those who want to change the country's employment patterns often believe they must also change deeper cultural values.

In an effort to get nationals to "grow up," governments are beginning to communicate that nationals' attitudes about work and service need to change.[94] One way governments are trying to deal with underachievers is through universal conscription. Both Qatar and the UAE have recently adopted mandatory national military service for young men. Those who drop out of high school must serve longer than those attending university (more than twice as long in the UAE).[95] The move is both a reminder to young Qataris and Emiratis that they have a duty to contribute and a jobs program that can provide training in the soft skills and discipline that underachieving youth may lack. Officials in the UAE have explicitly stated that apart from the immediate goals of bolstering the ranks of the armed forces, the national service initiative ultimately aims to strengthen the spirit of citizenship in the country and support labor nationalization efforts.[96]

In Saudi Arabia, while there has been no move toward conscription, policymakers working on employment are trying to push back against a couple of harmful perceptions—the perception that Saudi nationals are uninterested in work, and the perception that manual labor and service work are undignified. They cite historical example to show that perceptions can change: "Thirty years ago, there were not these values," one Saudi policymaker said. "Saudis did all kinds of work. Now we just need to persuade people again of the value of work itself."

[93] Ridge, *Education and the Reverse Gender Divide in the Gulf States*, 142.
[94] The recent World Economic Forum report on employment in the GCC also makes this point, arguing that "the prerequisite for effective [education] reforms is the willingness of authorities to give up their protection of young nationals to some degree, giving the latter the motivation to take greater responsibility for their lives." World Economic Forum, *Rethinking Arab Unemployment*, 27.
[95] In Qatar, young men are required to serve for three months if they are graduates and for four months if they are not. In the UAE, high school graduates must serve nine months, while those who have not completed high school must serve for two years. "UAE Introduces Compulsory Military Service," Al Jazeera, June 8, 2014, http://www.aljazeera.com/news/middleeast/2014/06/united-arab-emirates-issues-conscription-law-20146872230517860.html.
[96] Ahmed Abid, "Nadwa: Al-khidma al-wataniyya tuthra al-qudarat al-askariyya wa tad'am al-tawteen" [Conference: National service enriches military capabilities and supports nationalization], *Emarat al-Youm*, June 17, 2014, http://www.emaratalyoum.com/local-section/other/2014-06-17-1.686056. See also @Watani and @UAENSR on Twitter and the official UAE National Service website at http://uaensr.ae/.

Change Under Way

At the same time that these tensions play out, change is happening, too. Both government efforts and grassroots mobilization are trying to alter the cultures around work, citizenship, and entrepreneurship in the Gulf. Initiatives across the region are starting to promote the idea that governments and citizens should celebrate risk, encourage public service, and push for more local creation of knowledge, including for future policymaking. Bottom-up efforts at cultural change often also seek to empower nationals to push for social change, while top-down efforts seek to cultivate loyalty and support for the political status quo.

Celebrating Risk

To counteract the forces of privilege and risk aversion described above, some educators and policymakers are turning to the idea of promoting "failure role models"—examples of people who have tried something new or different, met with obstacles, and either overcome them or had to experience and bounce back from failure. Many people who were interviewed are seeking to draw attention to the accomplishments of "national heroes" engaged in innovative entrepreneurial work.

Multiple projects highlighting experiences of failure—or struggle toward unconventional success—are under way in the UAE and Saudi Arabia. Recently, the region held its first "FailCon"—an event with Silicon Valley origins where entrepreneurs speak of lessons learned from unsuccessful ventures. Participants at the event, held in Dubai, spoke candidly both about their failures and about the cultural barriers to embracing trial and error that they had encountered.[97] One Saudi company is sponsoring the creation of a YouTube series in which Saudis working in fashion, journalism, logistics, and other fields describe the challenges they have faced and how they have overcome them.[98] The series also addresses the fears associated with pursuing unconventional paths. One video, for example, features young people questioning the assumption that they must aspire to become a doctor or engineer. The company also said it had put ads in newspapers intended to inform parents about career fairs and diverse career paths.[99] Similarly, the Emirates National Development Program (ENDP) in the UAE is working on a publication series that will highlight Emiratis working in the private sector.[100] ENDP staff argue that human capital policy should promote Emirati role models with diverse experiences—and not just the success stories.

For some organizations, a broader goal is propagating genuinely innovative and entrepreneurial behavior, wherever people work. One Saudi start-

97 Natasha D'Souza, "Learning When to Start Over: Lessons from FailCon in Dubai," Wamda, July 2014, http://www.wamda.com/2014/07/knowing-when-to-start-over-lessons-from-failcon-dubai.
98 "Tashwiqat #Silsilat Akoon," YouTube, April 23, 2014, http://www.youtube.com/watch?v=dhoV1x_CZbw&feature=youtu.be.
99 Interview with a private sector CSR staffer, Al Khobar, January 2014.
100 Interview with ENDP staff, Dubai, November 2013.

up founder argued that his company's biggest added value was in "creating people who won't accept mediocrity." He cited with pride the example of one of his young female employees: after leaving the company to take a secure government job, she returned because the government work was so much less engaging and challenging. Given the strong incentives Gulf nationals face to accept secure and lucrative public sector work, it is unrealistic to expect that many of them will abandon traditional careers in favor of striking out into new businesses. This is particularly true for the average performers or middle classes with more to lose. And in fact, many Saudis leave private sector work as soon as they have access to a public sector job.[101] But many in the entrepreneurial community believe that encountering more diverse stories of failure and success, and exposing people to new opportunities, could create broader social acceptance for those who don't wish to pursue traditional careers.

Encouraging Public Service

Jobs and schools aren't the only place to learn and teach skills and build character. Some policy analysts looking at the region see public service as another way to combat entitlement mentalities, raise academic outcomes, and teach practical skills, and they have recommended integrating a service component into educational systems on a wide scale.[102] More generally, a growing interest in vol-

unteerism both emerges from and feeds back into human capital development efforts in the Gulf. Different actors—from governments to entrepreneurs—are trying to channel this enthusiasm in ways that shift labor market outcomes. Volunteering can help young people develop their teamwork and leadership skills, their work ethic and initiative, and their communication and organizational abilities. Without overstating the significance of organized volunteerism, which still has yet to become truly widespread in Gulf societies, recent developments in this area are of great interest.

Volunteering for charitable or social causes appears to have grown more popular among young people in the Gulf over the past decade,[103] although quantifying the phenomenon and mapping its ebbs and flows remain difficult. One example of such activity is a volunteering program sponsored by the Emirates Foundation for Youth and Development, a semipublic organization that rebranded and refocused in 2012 to focus on youth, social inclusion, and leadership. This program reportedly counts more than 33,000 registered volunteers and has proven popular among young people as a venue for spending time with one another, developing skills, and giving back to their community.[104]

In Saudi Arabia, a surge of grassroots enthusiasm for volunteering after the 2009 floods in Jeddah tapped into young people's interest in contributing to their

---

[101] According to an official with Saudi Arabia's Human Resources Development Fund, 30 percent of Saudis leave their private sector jobs within three months of starting, usually in order to accept a public sector position. Carlin Gerbich, "Saudis Drop Out of Private Sector for Gov Jobs," *Arabian Business*, March 8, 2015, http://www.arabianindustry.com/construction/news/2015/mar/8/saudis-drop-out-of-private-sector-for-gov-jobs-4976686/#.VaQJ6fmm2Xd.

[102] Ridge, *Education and the Reverse Gender Divide in the Gulf States*, 164.

[103] Others have noted this phenomenon, including Smith, "The Contest for 'Youth' in the GCC."

[104] Interview with Emirates Foundation staff, November 2013.

communities and has spurred the creation of multiple volunteering associations. Because of restrictions on forming associations or NGOs (as well as surveillance of informal activities), traditional "third sector" or nongovernmental activities often appear in Saudi Arabia within corporations' social responsibility programming, where charity and social activism can flourish more easily because they occur under the patronage of the company's leader, usually a prominent and well-connected citizen. One company in the Eastern Province sponsors activities like fundraisers for medical research and treatment, which it says attract thousands of young people wishing to participate.[105] Yet new, independent initiatives are also taking root. For example, television personality Ahmed al-Shugairi, who has 7 million Twitter followers and is host of a popular show called Khawater, promotes a website called Ihsan that helps volunteers sign up for and coordinate activities.[106] On his television show and elsewhere, Shugairi frequently urges young people to take social improvement into their own hands. In Dammam, another public figure, Najeeb al-Zamil, has made it his mission to provide aspiring volunteers with an associational "umbrella" to help legitimize their work.[107] The rise of access to social media and the Internet more generally—the vast majority of Saudi youth own smart phones—has enabled connections to develop in new ways.[108]

The government may be joining the bandwagon. Last summer, it announced a new initiative, Sons of the Homeland, which aims "to serve Saudi society and encourage youth to adopt positive behaviors and to volunteer during disasters and crises through various specialized work teams."[109] The program hopes to reach 1 million Saudis by organizing volunteer activities and "patriotic programs and events" that reinforce Saudi culture and identity. Some universities, like the King Fahd University for Petroleum and Minerals and King Saud University, as well as secondary schools, also promote "service days" and are often hubs of volunteer activity.[110] According to the team running Saudi Aramco's traveling iThra exhibition, roughly half of their event staff at any time are volunteers, and there is so much interest in participating that the opportunity to serve is now competitive. Saudi interviewees agreed that this passion for volunteering among some youth represented a new social phenomenon.

Multiple factors motivate youth volunteerism: in addition to altruism, youth may be driven by a lack of alternative extracurricular activities (and subsequent boredom) or by a desire to spend time in an acceptable mixed-gender environment.

[105] Interview with a private sector CSR officer, Al Khobar, January 2014.
[106] See the Ihsan website at http://www.i7san.net/, and an explanation (in Arabic) of how the website works at "Mawqa'a Ihsan lil-amal al-Tatawa'i" [The Ihsan Website for Volunteer Work], YouTube, https://www.youtube.com/watch?v=14U3NuNhP5I. Al-Shugairi has promoted volunteerism on his show, and his Twitter account (@shugairi) links to the Ihsan website.
[107] Interview with Najeeb al-Zamil, Dammam, January 2014.
[108] Google's "Our Mobile Planet" survey (http://think.withgoogle.com/mobileplanet/en/) estimates that the UAE and Saudi Arabia had 73.8 and 72.8 percent smartphone penetration, respectively, in 2013. Among youth aged 18–24, the percentages were 91.1 percent in the UAE and 83.6 in Saudi Arabia.
[109] Sultan al-Barei, "Saudi Initiative Encourages Youth to Invest in Their Homeland," Al-Shorfa, September 11, 2014, http://al-shorfa.com/en_GB/articles/meii/features/2014/09/11/feature-02.
[110] Interview, Dammam, January 2014.

Religiously-motivated desire to do good works may contribute as well. But young people are also interested in gaining experience and using their talents; their enthusiasm may reflect a hunger for the kinds of experiences youth in other countries get through school extracurricular activities or after-school jobs. Whatever the motivations of young people taking up social causes, many see their participation as an opportunity for employers to identify and interact with youth who are motivated and eager to learn. Volunteer activities can also strengthen social bonds and inspire people with new ideas about how to tackle social challenges. More service and volunteer activity may be good not only for the causes volunteers serve, but for broader efforts to promote more proactive, entrepreneurial mindsets—and youth adopting these mindsets may in turn demonstrate even greater interest in volunteer and service activities. They may also prove more motivated, inspired, and equipped to organize for broader social changes—that is, changes to prevailing attitudes, norms, or policies—that would have political implications in Saudi society even if they do not touch directly on questions of political order.

Producing Knowledge Locally

Wider embrace of risk-taking and volunteering, if it happens, will bring a lot of change to Gulf societies. Further change could come through increasing emphasis on locally produced knowledge and policymaking—that is, on having institutions

> Governments are likely to face increasing pressure to allow local experts—not just the well connected, but those with the best ideas—to have genuine input.

primarily staffed by Saudis, Emiratis, or other GCC nationals studying their own policy dilemmas and designing their own solutions. This is happening more and more: local institutions working on human capital and other issues increasingly want to be able to carry out their own studies and research. Many interviewees emphasized that building local research capacity was a top priority for them and a key goal of their partnerships with international organizations. For a long time, foreign research institutions and consulting firms have played a large role in the policy planning business in the GCC, and policies and initiatives have sometimes been implemented in unpredictable trial-and-error fashion. The drive to move past this phase in Gulf countries' political and economic development is a sign that earlier efforts to develop human capital have been successful—the countries now have the local talent to feasibly carry out their own research and policymaking. If the trend continues, it will better employ human capital that exists in Gulf countries and create new opportunities for the proactive to try to create change.

The success of these efforts will depend in part on getting better access to information. Long-term and high-quality data on causes of educational and employment outcomes, student goals and decisions, employer needs, and causes of unemployment or underemployment are currently scarce or nonexistent, though efforts to compile data that can inform human capital development policies and strategy have expanded in recent years. Qatar's education and training strategy, for example, cites as one goal the creation of a comprehensive, accessible online database for education and training information and planning.[111] In the UAE, policymakers and researchers (including the Emirates Foundation, the Ministry of Labor, Abu Dhabi's Statistics Center, and Dubai's KHDA) are working to build informative longitudinal data sets on education, employment, and Emiratization outcomes. The UAE has also launched multiple initiatives to support studies and training in research and leadership so that public sector employees are better able to develop and execute effective policies.[112] In Saudi Arabia, various branches of the Ministry of Labor—including the Human Resources Development Fund (HRDF), the jobseekers' program Hafiz, and the Human Capital Development (HCD) office—are working to gather information more systematically and to design studies in new areas. The HCD office, for example, is working with the World Bank to study what motivates Saudi youth to work and what drives their career ambitions.[113] These initiatives, if successful, will fill a substantial data gap.

Some initiatives to better coordinate policy planning between government, education, and the private sector are also under way. The Dubai International Academic City, for example, has hosted conferences related to Islamic finance, health care, and tourism that bring together educational institutions, government officials, and employers to try to better align strategies for developing sectors important to the UAE's economy.[114] Joint public-private ventures for technical and vocational education like those of Saudi Arabia's TVTC (discussed above) link educators and companies. High-level conferences and discussions focused on education and human capital issues more broadly—like the World Economic Forum and the Global Education and Skills Forum, both held in the UAE in 2014—can help to connect leaders across different spheres. But merely convening is not progress. Advocates for education reform and entrepreneurship in the region complain that too often, attending a conference is billed as an achievement, and various ministries and government bodies have not translated their promises into clear policies or implementation. In a recent survey, human resources professionals in the region said their greatest need from governments was a clear definition of future nationalization strategies.[115] That message is starting to be heard. In the UAE, for example, the Federal National Council (FNC) has called for a supreme Emiratization Council to establish long-term policies and strategies.[116]

[111] Qatar Ministry of Education, *Qatar Education and Training Sector Strategy*, 12.
[112] For example, at Al Ain University, the government created the Public Government and Leadership Center to serve as a public policy research and training institute. This type of initiative dovetails with some of the UAE's efforts abroad, including its creation of the Emirates Leadership Initiative at Harvard University, which supports research, public policy education, executive education, and other training programs. See Belfer Center for Science and International Affairs, "The Emirates Leadership Initiative,"
http://belfercenter.hks.harvard.edu/project/64/middle_east_initiative.html?page_id=538.
[113] Phone interview with HCD staffers, March 2014.
[114] Interview with DIAC staff, Dubai, November 2013.
[115] Informa, *MENA Labour Market Confidence Index '14*, available at http://www.menalabour.com/.

Governments are likely to face increasing pressure to allow local experts—not just the well connected, but those with the best ideas—to have genuine input. But just as entrepreneurs face structural barriers, policy entrepreneurs face the challenge of opaque decisionmaking structures and lines of authority in governments across the GCC. Policy decisions and implementation can seem haphazard or capricious; changes may be implemented without involving the multiple government branches or non-government actors relevant to the reform; and a single powerful individual who is indifferent or hostile to a reform can have the power to block it.[117] Given this situation, there are incentives not to transition to greater reliance on locally produced knowledge. Foreign experts and consultants answer to the client, rather than claiming a stake in the policymaking process, so governments may prefer to continue working with them. But having invested so much in developing nationals who think creatively about how to address their countries' challenges, Gulf states will be looking for ways to take advantage of their skills. Doing so by giving them a greater voice in policy, whether through new advisory bodies, think tanks and research centers, or even elected institutions, would create space for domestic political debates and would allow discussions about policy to happen more publicly than they have in the past.

Looking Ahead

Governments are confronting the fundamental question of whether it is possible to shift the expectations and obligations underpinning their political systems without breaking them. Trying to develop knowledge economies buttressed by more individualistic, entrepreneurial attitudes will create tensions and shift expectations. Some of the more challenging consequences of spurring human capital development amid status quo political and social structures—frustration, entitlement, and apathy among them—will have political and policy ramifications. What those look like, how extensive they are, and how governments respond to them will be major variables in the region's politics.

Incremental Change, Closed Space

Social changes and outcomes of efforts to develop human capital occur in a closed political space where efforts to secure loyalty have heightened in recent years.

First, governments (some more than others) have intentionally worked to cultivate loyalty, gratitude, and buy-in to existing political arrangements. In the UAE and Qatar, for example, governments not only provide citizens with material benefits, they also repeatedly let them know—through outreach in schools, public displays of nationalism, and sophisticated public relations

[116] The FNC also suggested that the government create "financial and 'moral' incentives" to encourage citizens to teach or join the media, medical, nursing, and tourism sectors. Samir Salama, "FNC Wants Federal Emiratisation Councils," Gulf News, January 7, 2015, http://gulfnews.com/news/gulf/uae/government/fnc-wants-federal-emiratisation-councils-1.1437844.

[117] As prior research has argued, improving public policymaking and policy innovation across the Middle East requires broad steps to enhance receptivity to public policy discussions, create sustainable business models for policy institutes, create a supply of policy entrepreneurs, and find ways to reward success in the policymaking environment. See Jon B. Alterman, "Investing in a More Robust Public Policy Environment in the Middle East" (CSIS analysis paper, Washington, DC, June 2011), http://csis.org/publication/investing-more-robust-public-policy-environment-middle-east.

efforts[118]—how lucky they are to be Emiratis and Qataris. Thus posters in a women's university in the UAE remind young women that they are "daughters of [Sheikh] Zayed" (the founding father of the country), a role that entails both privileges and responsibilities.[119] The UAE now has a new institution, Watani, devoted to the study, discussion, and propagation of Emirati values, including volunteerism, and to conveying the meaning and significance of Emirati identity and nationalism.[120] The UAE's National Day celebrations, which laud the country's achievements, seem to get bigger and more elaborate each year. Qatar also has a National Day, which according to scholars was created "to commemorate the ascendency of a levelling nationalism" binding the country's various social groups together.[121] The Qatar Heritage and Identity Center—founded by Sheikha Moza to cement "loyalty and patriotism,"[122] also launched a high-level National Identity Seminar to produce recommendations to "reinforce national identity" in October 2014.[123] Notably, the event's press release concludes with a description of Qatar Vision 2030's goals for transforming Qatar into a knowledge economy, a project that is explicitly linked to the need to strengthen national identity.

In some instances, governments are looking for ways to field more citizen input into planning and services, to appear more responsive to citizen needs, and to expand participation, even though clear shifts toward democratic political systems are not on the horizon. The Saudi Ministry of Labor, for example, is working on a plan to systematically gather and assess youth opinions about work and employment to inform its policymaking.[124] At a higher level, King Abdullah appointed women to the Shura Council for the first time, and he oversaw the country's first municipal elections in 2005. In the coming 2015 municipal elections, women will be allowed to vote for the first time, and the voting age will be reduced from 21 to 18.[125] It remains to be seen what liberalizing steps King Salman might (or might not) take. In the UAE, the federal government has pushed an aggressive "m-Government" initiative to make its services more accessible via mobile applications, including one that allows feedback on government performance.[126] Police officers in Abu Dhabi will reportedly soon wear body cameras,

[118] On the UAE's efforts, see in particular the Twitter account of Sheikh Mohammed bin Rashid Al Maktoum (@HHShkMohd).
[119] Interview with a university professor, Dubai, November 2013.
[120] See the Watani website at http://www.watani.ae/Portal/en/about-watani.aspx.
[121] Ali Alshawi and Andrew Gardner, "Tribalism, Identity, and Contemporary Citizenship in Qatar," Sound Ideas (Summer 2014), http://soundideas.pugetsound.edu/cgi/viewcontent.cgi?article=40 02&context=faculty_pubs.
[122] "Vodafone Named 'Exclusive Sponsor' of Qatar's First National Identity Seminar," Marhaba, October 14, 2014, http://marhaba.qa/vodafone-named-exclusive-sponsor-of-qatars-first-national-identity-seminar/.
[123] Qatar Foundation and Vodafone, "Qatar's First National Identity Seminar Concludes Successfully" (press release, October 22, 2014), http://cdn.qf.com.qa/app/media/22765.
[124] Phone interview with HCD staffers, March 2014.
[125] Ministry of Communication of the Kingdom of Saudi Arabia, "Elections in the Kingdom of Saudi Arabia," June 24, 1015, https://www.saudi.gov.sa/wps/portal/saudi/aboutKingdom/electionsSaudi/!ut/p/z0/04_Sj9CPykssyOxPLMnMz0vMAfIjo8ziHd2dnYI9TYwM_M1DDA08Tc2djR1NDO3dfY30g1Pz9AuyHRUBgiuYmQ!!/.
[126] UAE Government, "M-government," http://www.government.ae/en/web/guest/mobile-government.

in part to "help if a complaint were made against a policeman."[127] In early 2013, the government also test-ran a new "youth parliament" program for Emirati students; while the elected bodies created through the program have no actual governing function, officials said that the program's goal was "to promote political participation" and teach students debate and conflict resolution skills while also "fostering values of loyalty to the homeland, [and] promoting community culture and values."[128]

The broader regional context helps efforts to cement loyalty and to work within the system. The examples of uprisings in Syria, Libya, and Yemen signal to many people that stability is not something worth risking. Popular support for, or at least acceptance of, authoritarian political systems may prove durable in the face of threats from extremism, terrorism, civil war, and economic collapse. Across the region in countries that did not experience uprisings in 2011, people may criticize the systems that rule them even while finding them preferable to imagined alternatives.[129] Beyond the threat of chaos, the fact that Gulf governments are (to varying degrees) affluent and able to provide basic services and opportunities to their people largely insulates them from the desperation and anger that fueled successful uprisings in other countries in 2011. Public polling reveals, on average, greater satisfaction with life and more positive responses to questions about the quality of daily life in the Gulf countries than across the rest of the region.[130]

In addition, governments have responded to the Arab uprisings and their after-

[127] "Abu Dhabi Police Officers to Wear Body Cameras," *National*, July 9, 2015, http://www.thenational.ae/uae/abu-dhabi-police-officers-to-wear-body-cameras.

[128] "Youth Parliament for UAE," *Khaleej Times*, January 4, 2013, http://www.khaleejtimes.com/article/20130104/ARTICLE/301049936/1002.

[129] Reliable data that directly confirm this assertion with respect to the Gulf countries are not available, but existing evidence suggests that it is a reasonable hypothesis. Public polling that is available for countries like Algeria and Jordan attests to the support for status quo politics in light of regional instability. In a poll conducted by Zogby Research Services in late 2014, people across the region believed that the region was worse off following the Arab Spring, except for those polled in the UAE. Zogby noted that "only in the UAE do a majority of respondents give a positive assessment of developments in the region and their country since the Arab Spring began in 2011—largely owing, in all probability, to the general state of well-being among citizens and residents in the Emirates." In addition, past polls conducted in Saudi Arabia found generally higher levels of support for government based on Islamic Shari'a (i.e., the current system) than for democratic government. It seems fair to conclude that similar dynamics are at play in other Gulf countries, although this cannot be concluded with certainty. On polling data from Algeria, see Robert Parks, "What's Next for Algeria?," CSIS Maghreb Roundtable, May 14, 2014, http://csis.org/event/maghreb-roundtable-whats-next-algeria; with respect to Jordan, see University of Jordan Center for Strategic Studies, "Public Opinion Poll: Some Current National and Regional Issues," September 2014, http://www.jcss.org/Photos/635478411873156800.pdf; for the Zogby poll, see Zogby Research Services LLC, "Today's Middle East: Pressures and Challenges," November 2014, 1, http://www.aaiusa.org/todays-middle-east-pressures-and-challenges; on Saudi Arabia, see Arab Barometer, Arab Barometer Survey: Saudi Arabia (2011; in Arabic), 6–7, http://www.arabbarometer.org/sites/default/files/countryreportsaudi2.pdf.

[130] In Gallup's Global Wellbeing metrics, for example, which draw on polling results for 2005–2009, the five countries of the GCC included (Bahrain, Kuwait, Qatar, Saudi Arabia, and UAE but not Oman) were among the top 12 countries in Asia in terms of the percentage of people deemed "thriving"; each also had a high "daily experience" ranking, a measure of how satisfied people are with their day-to-day lives. Among these countries, the UAE ranked highest (51 percent thriving), while Bahrain (32 percent) and Saudi Arabia (27 percent) ranked lowest. Apart from Jordan (30 percent), which outscored Saudi Arabia, other countries in the region all ranked lower. Countries like Egypt and Morocco (each at 10 percent) fared particularly poorly. Gallup, "Gallup Global Wellbeing: The Behavioral Economics of GDP Growth," 2010, http://www.gallup.com/poll/126965/gallup-global-wellbeing.aspx.

math with both carrots and sticks, effectively co-opting or cutting off avenues by which people might push for political change. Lavish salary hikes and bonuses in the public sector in several countries in the Gulf reinforce rather than undermine the traditional social contract, even as efforts to shift attitudes continue apace.[131] At the same time, governments have cracked down more harshly on political activism. Bahrain's repression of Shi'ite political groups, as well as groups calling for reform and human rights, is most notable.[132] Other countries have also arrested and imprisoned individuals for criticizing their governments, lumped all political Islamists in with terrorists, harassed family members of those arrested, and shut down space for citizens to organize and articulate dissent.[133] Given the lack of strong incentives to push for dramatic change in the face of these repressive measures, social and economic trends will likely evolve slowly, and the impact of these trends on politics will likely unfold slowly as well.

Potential Future Trajectories

Those politics could evolve in a few different directions. First, human capital development efforts may not be very effective and may not significantly change people's attitudes and expectations. The generational shifts described above may be limited in scope, and may not extend much further than they already have. If so, there would be no interruption in the "underlying behavior patterns and created dependencies"[134] that existing employment and patronage patterns in the Gulf have created. Essentially, the status quo would be unchanged—at least so long as governments could financially continue to meet existing expectations. As current patterns are prolonged, entitlement and disengagement could both become more pronounced, making future economic and social shifts even more difficult.

[131] Others have pointed out that these salary hikes undermine the governments' own goals of realigning incentives to get more nationals into the private sector. In 2015, King Salman gave workers in Saudi Arabia a two months' salary bonus. In 2011, the UAE granted salary increases or bonuses, some as high as 100 percent of basic pay. Qatar granted 60 percent increases in salaries and social allowances to civilian public employees and 50–120 percent increases to military personnel. Saudi Arabia both boosted welfare spending and increased the number of available public sector jobs. Ben Hubbard, "King Salman Unleashes a Torrent of Money as Bonuses Flow to the Masses," *New York Times*, February 19, 2015, http://www.nytimes.com/2015/02/20/world/middleeast/saudi-king-unleashes-a-torrent-as-bonuses-flow-to-the-masses.html; "Salaries of UAE Federal Staff Raised 100%," Emirates News Agency, November 30, 2011, http://www.emirates247.com/news/emirates/salaries-of-uae-federal-staff-raised-by-100-2011-11-30-1.430917; "Qatar Budget Surplus Narrows to $14 bln," Reuters, July 12, 2012, http://www.reuters.com/article/2012/06/07/qatar-budget-idUSL5E8H726020120607; Mourad Haroutunian, "Saudi Arabia Creates 300,000 Jobs Since June, Eqtisadiah Says," Bloomberg, January 23, 2012, http://www.bloomberg.com/news/2012-01-28/saudi-arabia-creates-300-000-jobs-since-june-eqtisadiah-says.html; David George-Cosh, "Saudi Arabia to Invest $500bn for Bright Future," *National*, November 9, 2010, http://www.thenational.ae/business/economy/saudi-arabia-to-invest-500bn-for-bright-future.
[132] See various concerns documented at Human Rights Watch, "Bahrain," https://www.hrw.org/middle-east/n-africa/bahrain.
[133] On such developments in Bahrain and Kuwait most recently, see Kristen Smith Diwan, "From Parliament to Prison: Leading Gulf Parliamentarians Sentenced," Arab Gulf States Institute in Washington, June 24, 2015, http://www.agsiw.org/from-parliament-to-prison-leading-gulf-opposition-politicians-sentenced/.
[134] World Economic Forum, *Rethinking Arab Unemployment*, 27.

A second possibility is that efforts to develop human capital will be effective at changing how people think about work and productivity, and will in turn lead to change in how people think about their social and political roles. The outcome would not necessarily be some sort of violent uprising or Big Bang. Political pressure might appear in liberal forms: volunteering organizations could morph into more socially and politically engaged civil society organizations, and youth activism over social media could create new outlets for sharing stories of blocked opportunities, discrimination, or frustration with government performance. Some of this is occurring already in Saudi Arabia, where multiple government officials, including one minister, have recently lost their jobs after doing or saying politically unacceptable things on Twitter or in videos shared on social media.[135] New movements might push for social change, for example to root out corruption and discrimination, or call for greater policy transparency and coherence, or seek to shame governments into expanding political participation or addressing human rights abuses. People would continue to look for new models of how to question and persuade authority, even if no dramatic political upheaval occurs.

Political pressure might appear in illiberal forms too. Frustrated or entitled nationals could call on governments to adopt harsher policies regulating expatriate labor, which might put domestic political pressure at odds with international efforts to improve treatment of migrants. Or citizens could advocate for preservation of conservative social norms, forcing governments to defend their status as guardians of social order. Gause has argued, for example, that Kuwait's comparatively participatory political system has actually made Kuwait less open to laws and policies that could be seen as contravening conservative Islamic norms, such as allowing gender mixing or musical performances at hotels.[136] Educational initiatives and training programs that stress the importance of upholding national cultural and religious values, preserving national identity, and expressing loyalty to current governments reinforce the possibility that illiberal attitudes might become more powerful.

A third possible outcome is a significant shift in attitudes toward work, careers, and economic roles without much change in citizens' propensity or willingness to pressure governments to change policies or expand participation. Government efforts to shift economic expectations while instilling political loyalty, gratitude, and acquiescence could be fairly successful. Noting that interest in volunteerism seemed to ebb and flow, for example, one Saudi entrepreneur observed that "there are lots of obstacles [to starting something new], and most people prefer a safe and risk-free path." An example of how this trajectory might emerge is what happened in Singapore, where despite limited political freedoms, the ruling People's Action Party and former ruler Lee Kuan Yew in particu-

[135] Most prominently, the former minister of health was sacked after a video surfaced showing him acting arrogantly toward a man. See video at https://www.youtube.com/watch?v=j_vLfgrONT0. "Iqalat wazir al-sihhi al-sa'udi," BBC Arabic, April 11, 2015, http://www.bbc.com/arabic/middleeast/2015/04/150411_saudi_health_minister_sacked. For a broader discussion (in Arabic) of the expanding use of Twitter as a means to hold government officials in Saudi Arabia accountable, see Khalid al-Shaia, "Twitter mansa li-muhasabat al-mas'ulin al-sa'udiyin," Al-Araby, June 8, 2015, http://www.alaraby.co.uk/medianews/2015.
[136] Greg Gause, "Oil, Parliaments, and the Future of the Gulf," CSIS Gulf Roundtable, April 16, 2015, http://csis.org/event/gulf-roundtable-oil-parliaments-and-future-gulf.

lar helped instill what has appeared, so far, to be a deeply compliant, ordered, and growth-oriented society and political system. Perhaps unsurprisingly, officials in the Gulf often cite Singapore as a model they would like to emulate.

Conclusion

For governments to meet their own goal of fostering knowledge economies, they must sufficiently change people's attitudes so that they demonstrate independence, critical thinking, initiative, and willingness to innovate. Many people in the Gulf already have these attitudes, and they want to create change. Based on the populations' frustrations and expectations evident to date, actually changing Gulf economies will require that local governance allow more space to accommodate these new actors. That would mean further embracing steps that celebrate risk taking and even failure; encouraging cultures of service and volunteerism; and enabling the emergence of local research and policymaking capacities that can have a genuine influence.

Success on their own terms would also require that governments focus more of their interventions on the average and disengaged to expand the pool of talented and motivated individuals and avoid creating alienated, youth. No matter how innovative and hardworking a small elite may be, they will face obstacles if they are supported by ineffective institutions—in which jobs are considered an entitlement, training is poor, and incentives to improve performance are few.

Grassroots actors will continue to face the challenges of how to maneuver among shifting lines of acceptable and unacceptable activities, circumvent social barriers to new initiatives, and navigate bureaucracies that might either adopt and expand their efforts or stifle them. Successful grassroots efforts to build youth skills, promote public service, and encourage entrepreneurship are likely to be those that emphasize their contribution to the knowledge economy project that governments have trumpeted, or that downplay any potential political dimension to their work. Explicitly political and anti–status quo groups and activities are less likely to gain significant traction in the near future.

Efforts to change social and economic culture will come into tension with imperatives to keep politics as they are. The strategic goal of efforts to develop human capital—from the government's perspective at least—is to socialize young people to expect less from the state, contribute more to society and the economy, and do both without challenging the political status quo in disruptive ways. Evolution in how people expect to participate, to have a voice, and to create change in their societies is already happening and will continue to happen. Even without a social and political Big Bang, that change matters now, and it will matter for years to come.

[15] The Economist notes that authoritarians often "draw the wrong lessons" from the experience of Singapore, which "offers a real challenge to the liberal notion that growth, prosperity and freedom go together"—although the continuation of current trends there is by no means guaranteed.
"Lee Kuan Yew: The Wise Man of the East," Economist, March 28, 2015, http://www.economist.com/news/leaders/21647282-authoritarians-draw-wrong-lessons-lee-kuan-yews-success-singapore-wise-man.

About the Author

CAROLYN BARNETT is a research fellow with the Middle East Program at CSIS. Her primary research interests are in the political and social dimensions of economic policymaking and economic grievances across the Middle East. In researching and writing this report she traveled to the United Arab Emirates and Saudi Arabia. She holds an M.Sc. in Middle East politics and an M.A. in Islamic studies from the School of Oriental and African Studies in London, where she studied as a Marshall scholar. She also spent a year as a graduate fellow in the Center for Arabic Study Abroad program at the American University in Cairo on a Fulbright scholarship. Ms. Barnett holds a B.S.F.S. from the School of Foreign Service at Georgetown University and is a former editor-in-chief of the Georgetown Journal of International Affairs. Beginning in the fall of 2015, she will be a Ph.D. student in the politics department at Princeton University.

www.ingramcontent.com/pod-product-compliance
Lightning Source LLC
Chambersburg PA
CBHW081437270326
41932CB00019B/3242